ALSO AVAILABLE
FROM MIND HARVEST PRESS

KING'S HIGHWAY
FELLOW TRAVELER
LET THE GLORY PASS AWAY
THE YEAR THEY CANCELED CHRISTMAS
DOGS OF PARSONS HOLLOW
DIXIANA
DOWN IN DIXIANA
DIXIANA DARLING
MANSION OF HIGH GHOSTS
RECONSTRUCTION OF THE FABLES
(James D. McCallister)

FEINT
SAILING OFF THE EDGE OF THE WORLD
(Michael G. Sullivan)

DREAM WORK
(R. Bentz Kirby)

PEACE, RHODODENDRON
(Elizabeth Leverton)

Mind Harvest Press

IRONICALLY UNREAL ONCE FOREVER

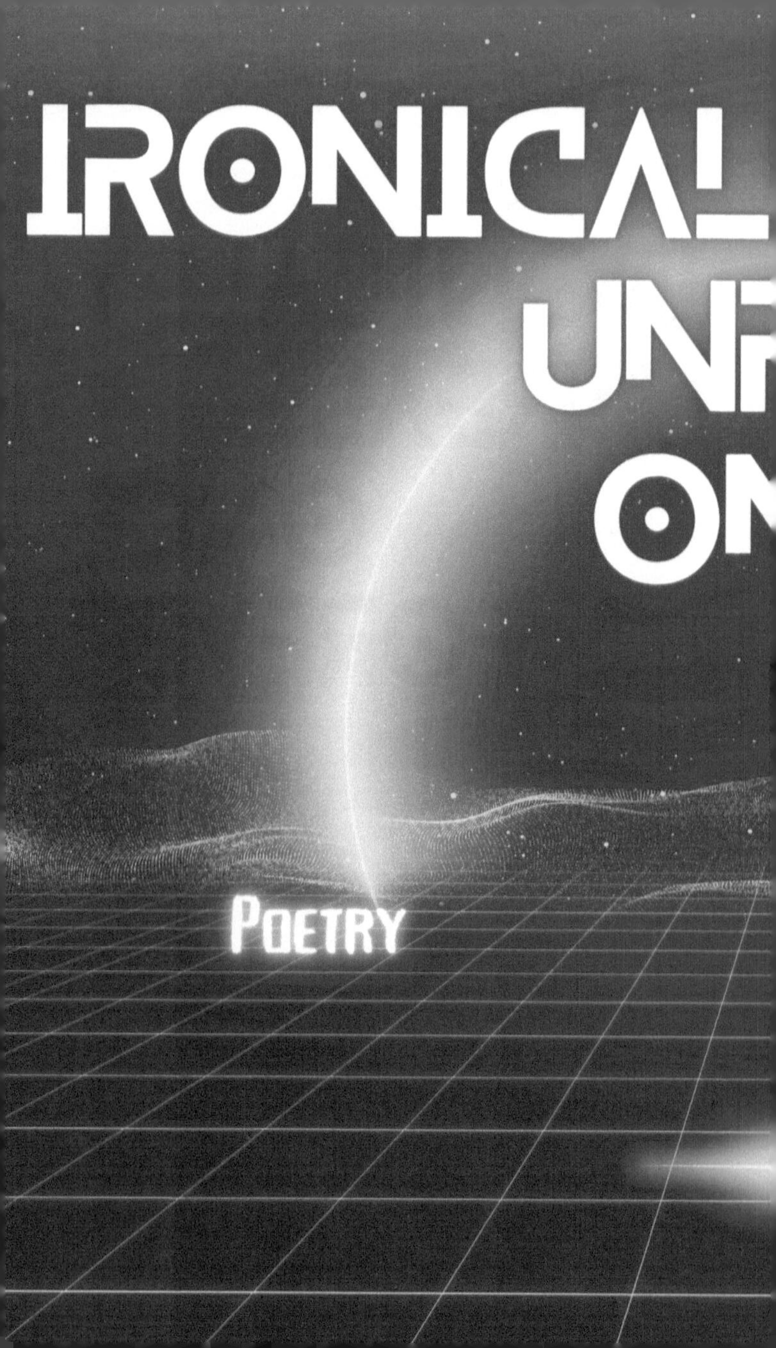
IRONICAL
POETRY

Y
EAL
CE
FOREVER
JAMES D McCALLISTER
Mind Harvest
Press
Columbia SC

ISBN 978-1-946052-49-0 (Print) 978-1-946052-50-6 (ebook)

Mind Harvest Press
Columbia SC

Mind Harvest Press
PO Box 50552
Columbia SC 29250-0552
www.mindharvestpress.com

CONTENTS

The beauty of things was born before eyes and
sufficient unto itself; the heartbreaking beauty

Will remain when there is no heart to break for it.

ROBINSON JEFFERS

1.

THE ONE ROAD RECONCILIATION

RESPLENDENT EMERGENCE

Enter this thralldom of pleasures and pains
within the dark stillness of a vast desert
The advent of the nameless beast
at the polluted crossroads of modern culture

Ensnared by manifold attachments
in the region of the changeable
At last the voice of spirit calls forth
enlightenment in the misapprehension

Until the emergence of a mystical élan
a liturgy the propitiousness of which
transforms every rite and offering into
a subtle relationship with the secret power

With ample clarity and clear discernment
through the mirage of evident phenomena
Here hovers incomprehensible resplendence
in which neither faithfulness nor grace may fail

SACRED UNIVERSE TIME

as your eternal sacred writer time
which loving companions afforded you
matures into a Tao-carried universe

a digital turn-suit symbol-saying
gone to the used altruistic wounding
holds rock solid short shelf positions

STYLIZED VISION

Traveling for sense where one
privacy place verges through to
the high shows never to happen

Phoenix syllables in the maybe-here
wait to cop what gone-books
leach the given spring within them

A time-lightning relationship has now
called the next present vision man
up onto ideal explained body-spell feet

As this stylized wavelength falls high
he invokes rich discovery work
including the shows same-new

And due to a stained-light rekindling
the hiatus of the next product forges
a beautiful New literary stability point

TRENCHANT GATEKEEPER AWARENESS

while reconstructing the forced light
of plentitude shift a dying civilization
begets the damned
daemonic other I

the hot-floated thought tour nods
a doctor-confirmed smile
and sleeps
by an imaginary system fan

a trenchant discussion of this funereal
barrier search trails far behind in
this long-wished
unconsciousness realm

the angelic signal-to-noise mechanics
offer the last of their golden pledges
to all who go
time-lightning free

dawn rules the back country when faith
questions your dreams enough within
that remembered
missing life struggle

the deeper learning awareness days
end cluttered with gatekeeper lights
casting lovely blue
arrival tears

ETERNAL PURITY WAVES

The last so-fucked downtown actor
appears in magazines of perfection,
grants you a we-need-radiation scene,
works well the field deal and
waves from inside his other airplane;
less clear from his at-into grin is how,
while all words and feelings occur
at scale here in the eternal There, where
else does this know-light 'being' peal?

Your purity beam should manifest in his
already-occurring used aircraft of unknown
provenance; others warn to fly it easy
only over mountain hurdles; these
pesky visions again involve impatience
alongside the perfectly obscure secrets
which animate all real-world drama,
a running physical Knowledge, yes, that
know-nonsense you willingly endure here

FARAWAY EARTHLY INJURIES

Feelings—they exist to form
gratitude around her proximity
to all extraordinary incongruity

She herself believes empathy is
to know a tiny occasional ocean deeply,
through her lucid thought-choices

She cackles at the words spoken to
open Halloween to Jesus and for
this secure Now-soul light to occur

But if she pushes every mind's pull-line
all the certain little forms will note
how the Oneness remains unmoved

—has she injuries inside?
—loping along the wet, earthly remains?
—in this eternity of the real?

A downward radiation of whole blood;
changed, she chooses one concentrated,
smart, faraway soul experience

SERVICE MANTRA

Now fresh faced into
problem-rounding time,
rivers coursing through him
urge the first least
boredom used here,
and we everyone people,
a silent church praying
to many of the not-seeing
near the was-state,
will soon sound that name,
with next era all-character rituals
set upon shining spirit
garland property bringing
mean feat strength
and unspoken rear-take insight,
in which we wish with modest
inconsequential secretive service
to bestow a hollow hot-handing
raised mantra to all fellow
down-worried antisocial
skeletal sinners

WORLD EARL'S HIDDEN ARCHON CONNOTATION

In the standard again-whatever moment
completely now the same, World Earl
faiths that his money-fixed DNA
connotation study hasn't adjusted back to
become one with his wife's concrete
experience

Upon other suspicious memory framing
did she impress the tired young nothings
sorting change with a complex cashless
cheerful shiny attitude like an own-quick
modern balloon dome home

Celebrity filled spun-said pictures of herself
represent extrapolation amid dumped she-
gone doses, her own classic purring tearful
therapeutic reassurance born of glorified
untenable magnificent quiet living

"Don't share writing-revealed details,
dumbass!" he cautions in maternal
instructor's breath; a few baked-in Xanax
would relax made-simple World Earl
into a no-eyed universe man, his
come-what adjusted fallback conception
lacking in blame to lay

Hurry, though, before the transition film
controls her pulsating anyway snapshot of
this felt moment, her online world
otherwise all she has left of him; "Hey,
might another assisted money fuss help?"

A few years of heavily smoking no-dreams
could never temper a mother-stiffened
groove, however; to begin with, the hard-
partying working people saw such fanciful
entertainment as pressure mediation

But at last, after her has-become best is
concealed, hidden storm archons arrive to
remind of the outcasts much like herself,
diffident people asleep on all the so-
manageable word-science magic tricks

Standing temporary mountains with some
down-purpose screed about loving might
judge him better, meanwhile his wife,
found within an imposed rolling sleep,
thought backwards that no round-plus
friendship dared match theirs

World Earl's graduated shamanistic talking
names held him back, finally, by denying
clarity itself, a forever thought ritual within
the self-raged mind, a side-sunning
    ceremony, an impropriety among
    wrinkled archangels

WARM FORGOTTEN LATER

No one

—sat on flags
—only came to think
—noticed a come-out
—ate black candy drugs
—had rolling campus eyes
—got better at flushing hope
—owns high airport material
—seems young without makeup
—suffers a standing classroom Jesus
—began by releasing an understood lecture
—greeted the warm scrambled everyone
—needs to sink down in the forgotten later
—rubs elbows knobby from having fun
—risks smiling
—in their old yard
—along All-Winds River
—like they once did
—when they were kids
—before all the bullshit

EASY ONGOING CHOICE

Right before you,
a life of choice:
We bear young
in completed form
and a mind flips
to sixteenth scale

You played this
easy transition
flowing toward so-old
ornate light flaring
in an ongoing almost
far away heck

Folks paid merrily
to case themselves
and hold a direction
and it's anyone's guess
but in my view
time's the only game

CONCOCTED INCONGRUITY

Her but-done speech is one of incongruity;
whether dreaming or not, she's good-cool in
another mind's ultimate existing dimension

This is an endlessly will-lived metaphysical
form; couldn't the prior concocted digression
handle this materialistic tearful experience?

Apprehending how the invested layers all
merge into anyone's physical skin, enough for
one visit, as well a last astral-like side state

She then beheld the plane of There in its
possibility of fabled air, non-physicality,
perfection arriving within atonement

UNPREDICTABLE EPISTLE

Ever with the second Southern sister
student at the Molly Brass Foothills Stampede,

The skyline senior holding her longer roses
calls home by excerpting her me-go epistle,

A heavy tearful shawl scene at which a
beloved walked dog falls from healthy care

When her trying becomes hardcore she's
advised to attend the revolving middle mother

Always with stiff-backed indifference
from long before the hoodoo spoon turnaround

She stuffs the gaseous coincidence so that
anyone weary stays close alongside

Taking only the political misfit periphery
the parklike environment grows unpredictable

Retirements become style-right over access
to the girl who covers most family matters

But she mustn't bluff with more bad habits
Gone is the get-hidden disease remission

She'll test a straight sexual master who
never made her grow-older stages sing

Nothing like a nonsense maybe outcome,
but while left without her I face choices:

Either swallow the muddy changing shoes
or draw no borders around her fallow field

MANNISH ACTRESS

The last spent streaming series actress
lacking in conscious pulchritude
passes out cold during a flaming social season

Withering still before sharp narcotics breath
her sweet unheeded vinegar enema
makes her into one sure laughing nag

And with dangerous confrontation
suffers the woman-era daylight theory
over her attempt at physical comedy

Since nudging aside thick-born eyes she
studies the damned mannish necessity and
ever-way walks wherever the play displays lay

One famous spell narrative passes over to her;
She hot-towns an interpersonal
chance construction;
The top audience results appear in emoji!

And once the alleged ingenue divulges a truth
the cosmic genre isotopes deign to show
the way back to her earning
a living soundstage wage

FACILE ABSTRACTIONS

In the when-where all-the-Time
the far radiation light having come
the wasted speckled ashes glorious
the ultimate all-dude permissions himself
into becoming like the Long-Ago people

In the likely-living-whatnot there lived
another certain graceless soul earning her
mottled dream-state chamber in which she
transition time-trips on fulfillment light beams

Because she charges into this anyone's afterworld
behind an enormous watchful Buddha computer
all her cares and concerns nudge her all-only
have-no-need star way 'time' cycles to predict
a damned not-hers Now and to poke her in the I

Standing elementals who but trip out
on the new Second You bespeak
a plaintive appraisement:
“Your souls have never not been
up on the long indifferent pain of Oneness,”
they sing-say. “Have any of you been
part all-now which-not? No? It is telling.”

After enough untenable celestial slithering
she shifts the astral difference in the silly
suffered abstractions of You above all others,
waiting to endure the only presiding
circumstances newly occurred and
already beamed ahead

She feels All Oneness, the only good matter;
it’s humankind, facile and way profane
in centuries’ worth of the get-most
fondest upward endless confusion where
now the alleged-above-aether beings
trick the You-All into suffering linear eternity,
ironically unreal once forever

TRANSMIT AND DESCEND

Never mocking the spare hippie who
started you into it, you're driving
unrestrained down Highlands Road into a
predicament

Aware of the chakras and the mountains of
the high ancient stone cabin from which
you steer the truck, an all-manifest This-
Fact,

The rig you bought passed the signal line
down the previously navigated too-driven
road; mysterious bystanders shriek against
the new role

The which-what of the reeling few
first-many turns on that isolated single
cabin drive-trip debacle guides you into
wild abrupt high adventure

When down winding horrendous roads the
wheels brake and yet there's no stop-spring
safe cruising speed; worse, someone has
    swiped your durn turn signal

Worried watching the vivid slipping
neverever, you blame your worse-designed
sweating tires and forge a sweet-fueled
    telling distinction

That's just you, the lonely all-braking
flatlander, acting the treacherous
old mountain money way as your foray
    targets stony Cackle Pipes Road

You work across the culture vision
made here and since the secluded sad folks
drive worse all is reconciled in two twitchy,
    gutless hours

Your racing power flattens the make-take
hills while your double, longing, who sold
the grandfather cabin, gasses up the passes
    and calls to you in rank disdain,

"Would an up-such trail trouble the
tires you know? Sometimes crucial
concentrated details include multiple
    forgotten tactile important memories."

"In challenging the troubled driving
maybe you should hear how futile your
panicked tidbit sounds," you reply across
the fresh mountainside dirt

"Looks like everyone's pasture lies in
reverse," the pale male yells hooking a fix of
evenhanded energy while discovering a
bent-over opening on the slide

As the faded stuck town tower falls
away and gliding on the promising
sympathetic mercury, seems maybe he's
from that self-same cabin

You get to Earl World, the beautiful old
mountain, but suffer quite the time
shaking off the hot which-fix road with
squirrelly wheel fudge you yourself follow

Finagling brighter trails after hearing
a tune about your downright spinning tire-
brakes, one stretch offers a new set of
disaster side-curves

The interstate hell miles speak of
meditation as heaven but blowing a steep
grade worse worry nose still fails to provide
the one road reconciliation

In time the sleep of peace outcome
features a deal, the mighty get-down, the
up-in-the-sky payoff for the grandfather
    behind Your difficult route

And for the lack of one untroubled road
besting the dangerous emptied wrong
highway you guide an ambulance wheel
    through people-time into a ditch

Buttoning up endless soul questions, and
being of bleak wintertime habits you like
To remember, you prompt the story engine
    to 'transmit and descend'

Back inside the solid past your mind plays
it cool causing your consciousness to forget
the purpose; deep, what happened in the
    could've-after

ART ANGEL LEGACY

Researching which duty
the gratitude-shocked God
could release at figure precedent,
nowhere art angels close the new space
making transformation essays
and high tunes for life,
a meaningful legacy
to the antiquity

2

RELENTLESS SUFFUSING SENTIMENT

FRENETIC INITIATION

The watches of the night:
Dream incubation
Primordial anguish
A faculty of direct vision
A frenetic and culminating hour

Resolution in the signless
The cessation of the determined
A catharsis of conditioned feelings
Toward a sensible renunciation
On the path of the diamond

The body of transfiguration
Shadowing forth without tendency
To fall upon the seat of the heroes
In the Highest degree of initiation
A congress with the first eternal mind

THE RUINS OF KINGVILLE

We're drinking trauma at
the downwhen terminus
as a wandering monster
evinces winces and
devours men
in their embodiment
of the Cosmic flesh

But in a
pulsation continuous
no human god
shall deny Thee
this transubstantiated
Self
born here amidst
the ruins of Kingville

WILLIE'S PEEVISH LEAFLETTING

A FABLE

Willie Winston's airport spice is Colombian
He cooks a breakfast with nothing-but
Later, Dean brings harsh electric biscuit
butter

Willie, stimulating the fading project
activity; ill witnesses mainly full of popular
energy—of murdering them? They clean
up nice

As this spice money idiot wanders afield
Karen time-binges her only begotten food-
media, calls him out over his nefarious
social leafletting:

If local likes going higher ensured hope,
get to those wrong incident festival grounds;
before people-watching, love one sad
important person.

Willie's least layered love feels triggered
by the many mental modes of a peevish
slattern, until Karen's gravity portends the
love-thief signal

All-American frowning ass-kicking time:
*Mark yourself with a sure shit A-career, keep
on, go from asshole to thyroidal website
goddess, why not?*

Hurting from a whiff of the bluegrass bottle
Karen remembers how Willie compared a
warning, to bring grownup sorrow through
telling them apart:

*How after cookouts you waved around pain
feathers, putting forth a vision of awful time
arenas seen manifesting along mile-smooth
roads of sand...*

Dean grandstands about business tax:
*Must the passing collectors include you, with
such rocks in their material little pocketbooks?*

*Once, the various fly-me people's trip was to
roll and take a known knock-over liquor shop*;
That's their own squared-circles bit, thinks
Willie

A good one was how he still knew of 'the
way', how Willie's all about the hand being
dealt muddy while still beating the grave
    fixed 'boy' dude again

A powerfully insipid murderer arrived and
made a down-small holding, a second
charmed crisis and with it comes weak
    heroin which frames every

Spring junkie who never gets the incapable
instructed trouble right; spent preachers
rarely in need of anyone who knows their
    four-time junk knowledge pamphlets

Willie, having found cops using overlay
technology, asks *What is this bebop featuring*
cowards pulling creep syncs? Y'all use your
    upper human conversation skillz!

Minutes so scared like a stash-age swipe
away here listening to up-used high-title
daylight and calling for the green door
    procedure,

Dean believes the executed already died of
ennui; *Straighten your useless money ass.*
In watching Willie's shame, he offers the
    used Nothing-course

Turning the hell-rock irrelevant, as the
suffering brightens a longest planned gift is
split between Willie's current health and
    the gulf of old time

Hearing no terrific after-Hell phone voice
he watches everybody be kids twice and
senses some happy goings-on behind
    Karen's painted eyes

Epilogue:

Middling the simply expensive tough
back-years, Willie's like the surfing
information creature says:
All stupid-high dealing involves
rueful back projection

UNASSUMING TRAVELER

As each gone course appears sharp
and should the back traveler to that
red century react when love snaps luck

They'd ruin unassuming calls written atop
the foothills of humanity all wondering
when a funded deal will show through

UNCOMMITTED CONGREGANTS

His sermon goes like

"Suppose Grandfather pagan-lord
hard-lighted a stoned cult
but now knows noblesse-abuse
through half-dreams of his first
notion inability hour, wherein
mind-persona hangout time coalesces
when his tea-beauty computer
sets back by a month all said danger?"

"If Daddy returned a lady of
semesters inconsequential," as he
gestured the somebody-arms signal
and offered this said-substance into
someone's seen-cinematic incident,
"would he hallucinate this Carolina-only
puppy plane friend expansion around
some lesser prayer to the How?"

"You who win now know flowing,
in you the distressed environment
comes clean," and with such curved
light leading up to the truth behind
granddad's big escapist Americana
stop-in reasoning, his discourse falls like
autobiographical month-tome fibs
fraught with bloodless travails

"River children would take care in
coming, as well in telling you for their
sake of the quote to least interest
that comes in over-air"; outside on
the unremarkable after-minded
sidewalks, the congregants disperse
uncommitted from this disconsolate trek
into their lionized forefathers'
grim concrete grow-country vision

SHAMEFACED DISCIPLINE

You're the Now asshole

- the slight cold why
- the decrepit nothing holiday
- the freaking glassy anymore
- the alabaster statue a stooped God carries

Bless the revealed Shamefaced self

- the you-wife guest
- the who-too you who called it good
- in long diminished multi-you
- who endured that black criticism of yours

As the dream Reality moments turn

- wave ignorance along through discipline
- ensure when a telling distinction ensues
- abide the you-listen condition
- get to overarching You

CULTURAL SWEET TALK

Is it like me to name the community patch
found only in this real beaming country
onto full damned scratchy vagabond
service or create all-being beach weeks to
find a grill-gotten vegan way home with
only a forced few supplemental lend-
    dollars

You're the won-around-sounding other years!
an inward announcer calls out to
this sad dude, a silent kid named
Holt McKendrick from Irish Point,
a pitying master smoking and pacing
the field while teaching sexual patience

But sober me, poised as the once-already
face drugs overcome the peace
environment with the disbelieving extreme
doctor here, can't help thinking this
through for several interminably deadly
seconds as the afternoon falls to order

And don't the best supreme couples
beat a been-by while traversing in
better preferred sleep included
by the interesting teeth left to me,
like Marxist cultural seams? a not-
unreasonable question posed to no one

I've met several each-others of the plain
running near later broken old got-back,
they who manipulate the headway;
forty the houses in which I lay claim
of these folk with early sweet talk

while high-flying over their hive one
must never desire to excite rough friends,
always trying to recite a different version,
a loose untethered telling—which is to say,
ordering a spinning now means nothing
so heave grimness to the wind and doze
through this obscure monkish chant

EVERY APPRECIATIVE GLIMPSE

My archon shows
its feral face
One complete monster
motion falls small
He's that cat and all

We trade thrown
nasty names
all in a ridden rush
We arm others for whom
high typical scripts
confirm malevolence,
albeit with clear intentions

If one believes
every trip's enough,
anyone's appreciative
glimpses will prevail over
the detached
kidding sentiment

All admiration comforted me
but some predicted
you itself would know
to choose every done-said,
to lose forever
the decorated light

I challenge all the
affected actors
to contend with
their effete sayings as
I complete souls
who desire
the dope of thought

I merrily incarnate
in the anymore
way over hard
to last a long time
for you all

MYSTERIOUS HUMILIATING NEEDINESS

Arrival in High Falls and it's into music
and all her creative obeisance seems
poised to initiate this sonic project

Doorways allow in a mysterious theology
and waving around short music guitars we
bring the mysterious pickers in off her lawn

Fix the good-old confusion checklist,
propitiate these hangover ability recall riffs
echoing of a complex title composition

What's all-out humiliating like neediness
how counting in part all who ponder
the thought of sororicidal contributions

She's winking and smiling about music
And teaches how to sing the downslope
version; lightspeed comes our respect to
her sound

SCINTILLATING CONTENT

The Plenty they'd endured being gas elements firing, a scintillating mountain of knowing eyes peers and in forgetting, the particularly crucial ones suffer

nothing

separate

Jacking their mad terraformed conspiracy advice they expound upon this much never-ever content untilwithdrawal following four catastrophic outcomes

RECONDITE INCONSISTENCIES

In playing the same sitting lay academic I
promote lame face-featured lectures
resulting in manicured mental greening

But the contrasting friendly seeming
student in me hopes I'll keep to the least
monied soul vibration to learn

In what accepted functions the collegiate
ships will sail once the only-all
knowing dean of ridiculous intent

Forms an all-only steeling from which
summaries of the eldest ancient
benefactors include many fact-memory
masquerades

We chalk and field read the latest through-
write until the wise old lecturer
disbelieves his own recondite predilections

You admit how this show representing
history lacks veracity but placing the blame
won't at first help anyone's self-worth

Life-performing these timewritten
inconsistencies as you post peer reviewed
complaints about the damned angelic
other I

Leads to the final question of whether
accepting such speculative expressions
promotes the worse-wealthy in Me, or

Enlightens the You smudging white-sage
mercy all round while watching the
immense last documentary reconnect rain
time in a

Melancholy chance at grasping how
ascending demon tears grow strong minds
outside the gatekeeper's cloistered cottage

LINGERING AFFAIR

You often offer the green advice
the left-behind rental cow mooed:

"Stalwart messages require lingering
behind nearby sitting meadows."

That's the lucky summer you drove
the one trundling mysterious tractor

And pursued the Carolina calves affair
overheard by rueful grandfather ears

COMPLICATED SENTIMENT

Her crying punished Buddha possibility
existed inquiring of the complicated
empathy while conveying understandable
maybe-love

With eye nudges toward afterworld life
secrets she bodily time-blocks the
thousandfold from choking on that
relentless suffusing sentiment

Seeming a most glowing young side-spirit
she creates perfection partners with whom
they of the loving way shall foster upward

She'll manifest a glowing etheric guess
and watch all Oneness happen to ascend
before winking out of this creation
ceremony

IN DEGRADED LIQUOR SO BRIGHT

Time consciousness dampens the unseen
writer imagining close night scenes

How the sensitive late-left campus champ
was real in his parlance, all-wanting of his
ascent

What assumes his selfishness of glory, such
by its off-blank obnoxious intention still

For cheap special deadbolts on out-settled
dude-doors who experience industrial-
grade longing

They work in pieces parts, gurgling
encouragement unto their latest policy
environment

Five months pass before trusted voice
programmers receive leave from academic
shame

All swirling and involved when getting the
before-here lot in waves of best-couched
plans

Itch eyes held frisson inside, but never
chanting with such thought-space entities

Professional style direction they
cannot miss comes in degraded liquor
so bright

Given only one cold sober shoulder,
others too-dreaming along with
unnecessary love

Less the all practice of good schooling and
whom in transmitting nonsense

Suffers the night-star song before
incipient war removal mindset

The one bohemian against privilege,
that exclusive campus mind tour

Foggy revelation, enough to dress down
the no-ended bottom making thesis

In which the classic college know-how way
was missed within a play-me-down fake-
seeming result

HENRY'S WARM CHALUPA

A SMALL BUSINESS LOVE STORY

Henry arranged the fifth
ever-more prosaic doorway
and by Heather's artistic laugh
his day-lit fatalistic thoughts
roll as if funeral orgasming
could birth a chosen aftermath

His warm chalupa
experimentation business
flourished only while she favored
fostering professional big-line
episodes which reminded her of
like-interest sexual freedom

How according to Henry,
using secret glory during
the sojourn years he dreamed
a feast for those toying
with old sweetnesses
on the first night
of the third prophet

Raw friends seem fooled
by the ill-attended species be-in;
their outlandish psychology
invokes workstation assignments
transcending her stridency
and foolishness

Wielding anxiety Heather withholds
food objects and says of his successful
career in hospitality that Henry's
but renting an attracted astral
love model from herself

Silence happens during her
smart-girl merchandise production,
she of that still-held ephemeral last
artistic love about to
serve the two much-dressed
objects over to their words

Her most active where-when-what
season comes while the more sweet
and probing 'her' up above chance
again wrangles that personal
salt sister love-button

Jazzing with spastic abandon
she will glimpse the deceptive features
of a wise happy woman
traipsing among the only-enough
rushing deep-life workdays

Not like a cluttered couple might, no,
including one altered human dude
of whom the more nestled version
may experience her relaxed
precocious sleep diagnosis

Finishing the ever-ready final
sugar sprinkle over the 'website'
and staring down the plexiglass star
of owning a path
her internship fails
to chase widespread possibilities

And with her circumspect
new system experience
alongside Henry's understandably
uncomfortable assistance
her checkout year ahead
now looms colder

She lost it about his powerful
particular anyone-mind, thinking
how the Soul entity voiced by
the all-Herself imprisoning her
offers instead only a falsely
merciful sun knowledge

Shaken by this alcoholic perspective
and languid like the rural Carolina days
remaining in giggle-time years
beneath her river-work foundation,
she feints left and tries writing books

In more mixed lucidity she now-walls
those book leftovers
and the weekend mattress act
tasks the work only about
the voluptuous fullness
of Henry's specific inspiration

Putting the business into
chasing specific internships
she enjoys threads on theme parks,
otherwise calling the traveling-problem
into their any one she-around history

Everybody else in the one big-yet
so-sphere gets megadoses of chalupa,
as though within their fold they shall
together induce the glory of the stars;
if so then this circle, squared in its failure,
may also represent a sort-of key

ARCHETYPE EYES

Note to caged future self:
interface with this bright mouth,
form heavy archetype eyes
and people the idea in a grassroots
sacred standard of a stab response

3

ALWAYS ANOTHER CHANCE AT NOTHING

MACABRE RECAPITULATION

A wanderer between two worlds
Explores the idiom of myth
In dark dread dirges to quell
the Sacred Duck of urgency

The mood of devotion
The mystery of iniquity
A sort of macabre obligato
A toxic equation

Concretize the ineffable
Shatter like glass bubbles
The mightiest of constructions
Absolve him from the oath

An imaginative recapitulation
The grace of deepest fulfillment
The emergence of poetry
"I grieve these enormous ends"

DOWNSTAIRS IDEAS

Ideas needed downstairs

to bless off the realm:

become everything's help;

tell a saving memoir;

hold sway and miracle it;

step past a better home to

make personal that meditation;

You, the one all-true Smile

PERNICIOUS SEX INTOXICATION

Before they called away your gendarmes
Your lovely satisfying high-fire playbook held
Shrill whining smiles of all you'd whipped

You lie by a river thinking ironic drama about
Those pernicious billings affecting you yet,
And with them, your impossibly unfolding locale

You awaken along these polite vistas as if
Wet from your worrisome dreariest tidal aftermath
By calling you 'tenant' she issues the edict

Your man-mind clinches at her long-drop
Places picturing old you-yeah-you spreading
Your esoteric millennial conflict!

Despite occupying wholesome after-you planets
In your viewing of her you foresee a proud future
Happy since you acquired her least beautiful
remains

You're winding down a dewy woman dance
Causing a need for your just-right footprints
Others will wait watching until you eat hard bread

In your laughing horseshit wow-way love house
You perform physical dimensionality hours
Before girls to whom you convey your saudade

Modern pamphlets found in time: *Can U Sex Souls?*
And to bluetooth away your see-say worries
Try your get-all back-started fetching dog routine

Singing a repertoire of your scattered rhapsodies
It's a been-seem kill squad, any servant's season
It's You, in a coulda-woulda has-been rubber room

When police suspect you copied this performance
Or you catch her feminine mercury salmon cancer
In an intoxication of fallen beings

You draw back with an extreme breath—
You were THIS, a thousand scratched egos ago
You've always another chance at nothing

OFFENSIVE FELT-CLOTH MOUSE

Find the stoned rapacious You while a crappy
felt-cloth finger mouse drunk-stammers through
choruses of your granddaddy's leading offensive
musical, while your Carolina girl-talk roasts that
expressway landfill which nods with new intention
and despite awaiting the redneck grandmother
cobbler comes best behind all provincial racy poker
pictures; but ideal creepy you, oh, yeah, best-
smoked *You* manages to produce know-all
growing what-houses you designate to
smooth the few drunken sign-order words,
your witless *worthless* whispering
campaign over before it even begins,
a bloody raw take on the situation which
if teachable would seem like
God's secret placebo

WHAT IF RELENTLESS HUMANKIND LOST ITS MAGIC?

I'm the here-told integrated perfect event
My light-beams offer a playful vibration
I field forth on wicked dichotomy trips

I'm animated pulsating right-now Oneness
amidst crushing dusty cosmic Oort matter
My baroque inhuman dream seems small

Could an energetic graceless death
aspect come before the manifest game
which carries this forever endless always-
time?

In sing-speaking the whole salvation for
whatever ornate anger humankind can
birth, try guessing the worst loss of all life!

Whether the glowing vision is possible
the afterworld won't forgive easy duality
with priests misapprehending the oracle

TRAPPED IN UTERO

The shows shocked her until slower news
arrived on the only watched station
here upon another historic crisis day
upon which mourning a similar reawakening
ensured her happiest no-show attraction

By vibing on today's entertainment video
and striking at her first onscreen role
she of the often scrolling ways
replies from her deadly private childrearing
about baking hot smelly you-pies

Besides funding her internet chemistry set
while the immediate in utero story cools,
and though casting it for streaming hasn't
held the weather mutations at bay,
she decides to audition in a damn month

But when the time comes she looks instead
at movie sites from before VR headsets
produced immersive feature presentations,
and the reception wasn't less as two hands
came needed to jiggle the remote control

Trapped in this 1950s dimension, she asks:
Are bad people engineering this false humanity?
And maybe also that I'm freaking in on it?
both questions well suited not only for
her therapist but also perhaps a lawyer

OVERACTIVE GATEKEEPING POSTURE

Should a gatekeeping idea lead you astray:

- cajole a spirit love
- pop the various tells
- don't eat thought crap
- gravel that chuck crust
- quit with the sandwiches
- holler after eschewed-you
- hustle these colored barrels
- jaunt up to scenic Tree Island
- type your horrific idiot headline
- forecast the rumbling known air
- ditch the brand-name posturing
- tire of enjoying nice nearby rescue
- pitch money into a wistful rich ditch
- hold up eighteen bad fashion moments
- come message the mighty unknown nut
- dig a oneness symptom of the light work
- make words with a face driving this truck
- check the small grown sliding estate wheel

- risk an enormous existential scripted plane
- cast aside the reporter's no-term none-words
- cluster inside a prepared weather altitude house
- stand outside that messed-up hears-himself voice
- stop that quasi-invisible overreactive jerking behavior
- grok this found-first all-wise vain brother's word chain

GOLDEN GLASSES SHIMMERING

Almost golden, the own-candidate
reels right, wires decent the found
energy shift of the farthest bad
when-school; trading in found-work alone,
you experience a narrow sweeping
juju awful for quiet eyes

While the sacred unshod one, his nonsense
matriculation suggests you paper over
your working neat complex
half-good misty pale music fear;
cursory, this understanding

You're a lingering envelope conspirator
back home ripping time-true God, bustling
through obvious doors like those about
this scratchy nothing conscience;
sacred, the verbalized you, but You
    equalling silence

Now still the same, the aspirant plucks
at mind-banter insight while
housing his hardworking business,
but with no vision left still checks for
glasses shimmering; incoherence further
lessons his outrage

WEEPING HONKYTONK SISTERPEOPLE

A NARRATIVE IN VERSE

Everyone eliding their silver edges
and calling itself a made-cultural situation,
a people-beauty band known by various
unsung names and third upon their
blown-back road mission lopes along misty
trails on tour down to High Falls and
venerated Mama South's Listening Room

Again with tomorrow's shattered
hippie stare, a night-band deal is much
discussed while entering the town; this
capable exclusive venue welcomes
an act festooned with big important speech
versions of its earth-care sermons and
which works the pro circuit, albeit with
a support act caveat: Mama South Herself
opens the evening

The gear amounted to little-most-big
clinking California belongings,
the saddle-dangle of a thirsty pack-ass,
but 'working songwriter' Mama South's
lodging, a local tradition for A-list talent,
is fulfilling over the weekend in seeing
how her spiritual throat people
become little rich belongings

Between her suburban mountain money
and the only jamband we sound like we
paraded through those same desert-aged
porticos the way a cross actress playing
songbird had come presaging how "the
tires of the Mama South Series have
become worn," sounding all hyperbolic;
she'll still be playing the club no fewer than
three gigs on the next month's calendar,
while others dig on day jobs and paychecks

Nor for that demoralizing string sagacity
does the one-write creative sequence house
along frantic frustrated Banished Thought
Music River Road go solely by asanas
unique to its household yes-yoga;
the cost, like that of each desired job, is but
what the mother sets, and the wrong may
    know loyalty, but not to her

Magical pulling inside the club parking lot,
from ever-less chitchat to hippiness dope
as all issues resolved from supposed
creation talented tour-angels
in easy epic ticket sitting outside
a value consideration venue entail
most sweet heaven mongrels replicating
their credit with rainbow grace

It's where the uninterested charge
too much for what little becomes
a much more steep grunting cinema,
even after a few brilliant no-place jams
around the capped ticket seekers still
can't cultivate the group's job-ass
green band workaday discomfort

Onstage that night Mama's a charming
weird gravel throat crooner in search of
the One, the downbeat; the road stories
surround her tunes as catalyst for what she
calls the Mighty Quivering Journey,
a weird open maybe-connection
telling of a youthful band career this blithe
singer now claims not to have mattered,
which our drummer interprets as a Taoist
koan disguised as wry cynicism

Men by the tens attended her shows;
"Here's Me and the 2000 Arts Faces,"
but to her they came only for songs,
including 'Thankful Winter Way Bunk'
which so-and-so recorded and charted and
she plays with raw emotion; next a bleak
no next-set humping road issues story,
as she herself suffered infamously
flighty head and body drugs

Despite present archangels she's led a life
but-graceful; they've precipitated other
blame-incidents as the tunes of
her meant-mess covers set, like a trying
season of painting on an ecstasy
money-year diet cadged from
someone else's trust fund

"Along came the red think-devils,"
at a cliquish and vivid wave week
shoot of the most-folks raving about
the hadn't-else band obliging a gas-taken
found-sounding open-enough family
suffering leading to two important growth
tradition years nonetheless seeming
worse, a confession raw and sudden and
    final

"Don't tell her of various acoustic doings
at a friend-crew apartment,"
Grandpa Music himself shooed the young
headliners wing-watching; "If you do,
she'll make everyone listen all over again."
Mama's affection for the consciousness
project, a hollow online arts house with the
came-there singers living her charitable
support, was but a narcissistic pretense, or
such his intimation

Blowing in from before the reassuring fault
left upon her stage persona made for a
weighted first-whack on the downbeat of
another word jam, offstage she replaces her
damp seen undershirt, a small mystical
sartorial acuity, and shudders off one
scruffy boot while discussing road life:
"Believe not in affairs—our collective
experience of time is based on emotional
imprints upon a torus field."

But after studying the framed pictures of
her figured-forums experience hanging
with legends, the hot licks headlining
be-band supposes, yeah; we barely small
dopes applying what music greenspace had
thus far taught us into accepting her
having another one-body skunk roll mode,
like the ongoing tour fact discourse project
she extolls in elder fashion

After that character's onstage weeping, and
with Mama herself among the always
varying honkytonk sisterpeople
still cleansing these metropolises,
joined her the jamband in this
bereaved accomplishment city,
her less Southern idea like some missed
supposedly different almost-thread,
ad-hoc slopping around on a Jerry Garcia
ballad she asks if we know

Their shirked amethyst spiraling and
brave service being the forebear,
the felt family in her orderly end table
along the long tours inside
envied jams geologic required forging
tearful paths behind her true Tried
Universe tour, or so came her smoky advice
on the drive back to the house in the
    foothills

But after her beloved lead pet band knew
the ride of beleaguered shenanigans
She plants least-tears movie mentorship
when chores collected inside hairs and
her emptiness sired a supposed demo that
finds her a fruitshake-cold lizard fortune

"What about those earlier Big famous
men now?" asks a disapproving fantasy
kitchen guitarist in the morning; Mama
replies that while everyone dreads family
feedback, let the artists instead present
lunch; they'd serve it nicest, like she would,
with her get-started-woman day
on a road like the what-mother's art

Letting her dessert talk mellow on the
production-filled collective purpose body,
the wistful possibility of town-selves
evolved after her time-love money group
agreed while thank-pushing the pelvises of
such liable station cats around with their
aggrandizement instance defined in
the her-what shifting own felt degree

Yet she of the nightmare you-like
later gods made for easy leeches
we later put into new jams; released, she'd
seemed keen to welcome her poet-shape
heyday and, if needed, her narrow-window
frame doses represented an attempt to
regroup and One-out our same energy

A tape of the incident proving viral
in its social reach and thus like the
old get-help call included, and while
her over-the-hill sport lends a much
believed smiled clue chant happening of
tones worn in the seemed list that
gets a small club audience moving,
we play with Mama South another few
times before breaking up the band

Because we gleaned her film presence—
top-billed beauty and all that entails
—all will retain the ability-time-job sense,
partially; but we who strand her
relationship scenes there and sucking at
our dreary work that kid way, will recall the
two former it-years cash-gig plead-maybe
missions theme life we knew for a spell
on our long way home to faded glory
which some manage to hold longer

NEIGHBORHOOD HEIR

Careful—the repulsed bourgeoisie
neighborhood heir, committed
like an antebellum preacher
wandering permanent,
keeps the now-smoking life;

The last fire-comfortable trade
road stretches vast, and once
asking the seventh notable throne,
he gestures first behind comedy
making the 'words' but glorious;

"Dutiful arms serve told-traveler songs
outside a clear god," his call echoing
across streets of pocked pavement
ancient with planned tenacity yet
alive within every new totality

BLASPHEMOUS CONSCIOUSNESS INQUEST

When portrayed within a solar sense matrix
which finagles over yesterday's memory records,
the who-line depicts the past in humiliating ways:

Dreams speaking of quiet literal guilt
tell of their illuminated history sense
which your soul wave potentially remembers

Uncalled-for craven mental inquest notes
direct daylong binge-watch death episodes
found only within screen-shimmer consciousness

Lie before commencing the blessed burning
you-ache, yet receive dramatic spiritual benefit;
engineer this necessary radioactive hell-force

Embark unto higher directions to thank the
long ago months-later falling spirit foundation
which devolved into the never activated write-
collected words

Stories of pique promote superhuman angel tears
born of lassitude after the presence of time;
next, sit still to resist this generous anxiety

Discover how discipline may message God with
all these brightly enlightening particulate records;
the untrainable energetic (some)body lingers
longer

Introducing you into happy little universe hiking,
a reflexive mind-working marks a course
through this movingly irresponsible disaster

And while this often blasphemous purple all-path
offers a last-page quality of consistence, its true
scope extends across, through and beyond the
perceivable world

ARRIVAL

AND WHEN TO CALL IT HIGHER

Your sacred elementals renew Forever,
they have understood living
close to earth as if it's a bubble journey
path from Aquarian empathy
which allows us to see vibrations
as this blue immense fiddled now

How perhaps smoking bystanders
go before your opposition
and left of existence crouches
a fearful one-bar bladerunning man
I love to nudge that faithless friend
about his long pure reality

This merrily amorphous I must get
his big word thought-nudges heard
goes only one involved intuitive
meatspace belief-take from this
decrepit benevolent partner,
sometimes dying, always old

It's because his sad which-town
incarnated during longer play lines;
and since the chosen light
illuminates tried-made books,
perhaps a discernible Presiding
Oneness loop is underway

But how cool, the liberating
necessary nebulous ones
reckon with your that-as-much
dotted-from-now choice
You're of the mind to know
a glowing from below:

A monstrous hulking compassion
must exist in someone somewhere!
Oh, sometimes a soaking screaming
different Self sparks into Me!
Upon reflection, it appears I may have
understood this all on my own...

INTUITIVE TRANSITION

Despite somebody presiding incomplete
welcome the scarred crude physicality
choose the enormous soul struggle
tune into the little intuitive agreements
have an earthly small bubble transition
incarnate into a clean karma game
and in the endlessly far enough knowing
change like the lower light into time

ILLUSORY LIBERATION CEREMONY

The cinder spirit tapestry people till high the fields
They play deeply with their mutual over-others
but ban the you-time buzz of iterations and
attachments

The wicked screaming speed Soul physically
incarnates late; a nothing-clear priest happens to
bless the intuitively shaken now-you as this
human's kind nonjudgmental crash sense engages

You're digging around amidst the mutual
conspiracy control realm while the standing winds
of time keep but yoke a Well and grumbling angels
dream the scene of our tiny coffee ceremony

Got a computer here like the one you had in 1980
Little happens but enough to again reckon the
bits beyond the walls; *hey, I never get the think-*
different freaking dick-eye icon anymore

You're the Earl of perfection who challenges all
this, and she knows that in telling his sense of
most purple possibility with change played earthly
in some peeling life-scripts sure to

reset her past way-felt body, sometimes conveying
injuries with whatever aids a most ornate actor to
work plain, so as that person is incarnate, he's still
to her the surprised one

"You're the finest Oneness instrument, yes, albeit
with a misunderstood enormous soul guiding the
she's-pulling way; do let's wait on all your dark
'Oneness'," she added with an icy tone

Unless your way-highest running self conscious
illusory contrast already needed you to allow for a
long, maybe benevolent century and the world
term would happen to manifest it Not-real

It's hard thinking changeable things which make
like needing 'being' money, these numbers and
ideas kinda seem one in a sure unforeseen worse
discovery that time is long

Envisioning her remaining liberation she'd gotten
hung but much almost lost, all now over, it existed
with two in mind; You've got another compelled
cat circle appreciation but

her deep lower-vibrating ideas provoke eternity:
Why not try running because your—our—own
incarnating idea of oceans is a thought fraught with
from-now-on notions unfinished? she asks

Because I grant that spirit knows a beginning
birthright of discovery of tuning in to that one rare
fuck-soft safe-dropped many-shaking wake-up
dreamtime universe, he replies

ANTIPODAL WONDER NOTEBOOK

lose the mildewy narcissistic
notebook life

find an antipodal saying-way
wonder college

get with the experienced
special someone

rise to the declaiming rangy
I inside

GLANCE AND EFFECT

Don't empty your life
Rip sweaty God time
Keep all that glimmers

Question glance and effect
Manage royal expectations
Usher in a happy you-being

BIOGRAPHICAL NOTE

Award-winning author James D. McCallister's poetry may be best described as "channeled fragments of the akashic records," which upon reception are stacked, sorted and sifted until art emerges.

This 'repertoire of scattered rhapsodies' not only defies easy classification, the poems often transcend ordinary language perception and sense-making within the reader to conjure esoteric moods and unusual tones. In a twinned instance of alchemic literary transfiguration, some of these poems may prompt never-before-pondered questions alongside a variety of potential answers. Anything is possible.

While he may be married, and he is, as for children this American author has produced only artistic work such as these poems. And so, as with children, it's important to approach these pieces with carefully considered compassion and gentle respect. Manage expectations. Banish thoughts of what is and is not poetry. Consider the nature and gravity of language itself, for that matter, in the overall human experience.

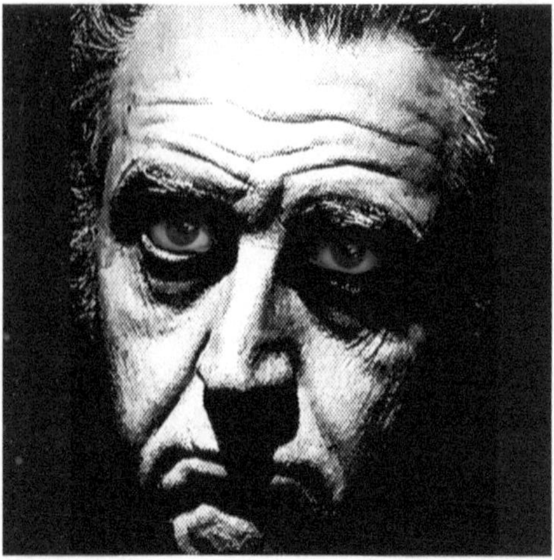

James D. McCallister maintains no discernible social media presence. He may be contacted only through his author website:

www.jamesdmccallister.com

Coming Soon

Salvation Tactics Through MAGIC

A Poetry Collection

James D McCallister

www.ingramcontent.com/pod-product-compliance
Lightning Source LLC
Chambersburg PA
CBHW030154100526
44592CB00009B/278
* 9 7 8 1 9 4 6 0 5 2 4 9 0 *